WHAT WOULD GRETA DO?

summersdale

WHAT WOULD GRETA DO?

An Hachette UK Company
www.hachette.co.uk

Summersdale Publishers Ltd
Part of Octopus Publishing Group Limited
Carmelite House
50 Victoria Embankment
LONDON
EC4Y 0DZ
UK

www.summersdale.com

Printed and bound in China

ISBN: 978-1-78783-616-7

Substantial discounts on bulk quantities of Summersdale books are available to corporations, professional associations and other organizations. For details contact general enquiries: telephone: +44 (0) 1243 771107 or email: enquiries@summersdale.com.

Disclaimer: This book is unofficial and is not endorsed by Greta Thunberg.

CONTENTS

INTRODUCTION

THE CLIMATE AND ECOLOGICAL EMERGENCY IS RIGHT HERE, RIGHT NOW.

GRETA THUNBERG

Instead of looking
for hope, look for action.
Then, and only then,
hope will come.

GRETA THUNBERG

Whether you choose to believe it or not, we are facing a climate emergency — if you've picked up this book you probably agree. The evidence to prove this fact is clear, readily available and backed up by scientists. According to 11,000 scientists, "untold suffering" will occur to the world's people unless major changes are put in place among global society.

The situation seems overwhelming and hopeless but there are things you can do, even if they are small, that will make a difference. If everyone were to think and act in the same way, we could make a big impact. This book takes a look at some of the issues behind the crisis, seeks to offer answers to a number of key everyday questions, and offers suggestions around what can be done to make positive changes.

One of the biggest lessons we can learn is that we should simply use less. We should think about what we need over what we want. There's an expectation that we should be able to have whatever we want, whenever we want it. We might even think we deserve stuff. But what's more deserving, making ourselves feel momentarily happy with something shiny and new, or making an effort to stop damaging our environment and building a future for our planet? It's time to slow down and think about our actions, to be more thoughtful about them and their impact. The first thing to do is to stop and consider what you do now and pick out some areas where you could make a positive change.

The Earth will not continue to offer
its harvest, except with faithful
stewardship. We cannot say we love
the land and then take steps to destroy
it for use by future generations.

Pope John Paul II

The Earth is what we
all have in common.

WENDELL BERRY

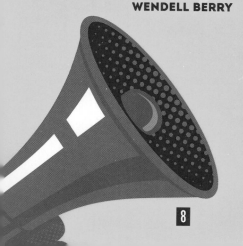

WHAT YOU DO MAKES
A DIFFERENCE AND YOU
HAVE TO DECIDE WHAT
KIND OF DIFFERENCE
YOU WANT TO MAKE.

JANE GOODALL

Never doubt that a small group of thoughtful,

committed citizens can change the world;

indeed, it's the only thing that ever has.

MARGARET MEAD

The moment we decide
to fulfil something,
we can do anything.

GRETA THUNBERG

HOW CAN WE EAT IN A MORE ENVIRONMENTALLY FRIENDLY WAY?

THE ONLY SENSIBLE THING TO DO IS PULL THE EMERGENCY BRAKE.

GRETA THUNBERG

The ultimate test of man's conscience may be his willingness to sacrifice something today for future generations whose words of thanks will not be heard.

GAYLORD NELSON

There are some easy ways in which you can make eco-friendly changes to what you eat, how you source your food and how you manage your food consumption. When it comes to the environment, a key consideration is always to think about what you need, rather than simply what you want. With a more thoughtful approach to food, you might well realize that you are being wasteful or that you've fallen into bad habits. A few simple tweaks to your usual routine can help you make a positive impact.

The same applies to food waste. Did you know that 1.3 billion tons of food is wasted globally each year? It is estimated that each person in the UK and the US wastes around 100 kilograms (220 lb) of food a year. The UK throws away 7.2 million tons of food every year, and more than half of it is perfectly edible. In the US an estimated 30—40 per cent is wasted, with food waste accounting for the single largest waste source entering local landfills. Meanwhile, one in seven people across the world don't have enough to eat.

EAT LESS MEAT

One of the biggest positive changes you can make toward helping the planet is to eat less meat. To give you some perspective, meat and dairy production creates more climate-changing gases than all forms of transport combined. A whopping 14.5—18 per cent of these gases are generated by the meat and dairy industry. Rearing, keeping, slaughtering and transporting farm animals for human consumption uses up a lot of resources compared to farming plant-based foods — it takes around 11 times more fossil fuel to produce animal protein than plant protein. Animal agriculture also guzzles far more water; it takes anything between 1½ and 6 times more water to produce a gram of meat protein than it does a gram of protein from pulses (like beans, lentils and peas).

Reducing your meat consumption or going vegetarian can dramatically reduce your contribution to "invisible" waste (the waste you don't even see throughout this process) and your carbon footprint. There's lots of information available online as well as recipe books that will help ensure you still consume all the nutrients you need, helping you safely and healthily go meat-free.

EAT SEASONALLY AND SHOP LOCALLY

Seasonality of food refers to the time of year when a given type of food is at its peak, either in terms of when it's ready to harvest or its flavour. By eating seasonally, you're ensuring that your fresh fruits and vegetables haven't been processed or transported long distances (from places where the food may be in season). Clearly, if food has not had to make a long journey — maybe by plane or boat — it has less of a carbon footprint.

In addition, the farther the food has to travel and the longer it has to stay fresh, the larger the amount of packaging.

It has also been estimated that between 20—40 per cent of crops are lost to damage while being transported. Food industries attempt to reduce this damage by piling on the packaging: shrink-wrapping individual fruits and vegetables, adding packing foam around boxes full of goods and keeping certain foods frozen or chilled, which uses up more energy.

If you can, try to shop at stores that stock locally grown products. You'll eat more genuinely fresh foods that have a smaller carbon footprint and generate less landfill waste to get to your table.

TOP TIPS
FOR FOOD SHOPPING

- Only buy what you need – don't get tempted by marketing offers to multi-buy when there's a risk that extra food will go to waste.

- Look out for food that's produced sustainably – labelling on products should help, and there's loads of information online to point you in a positive direction.

- Buy products that have been farmed sustainably and ethically, such as those marked with the Fairtrade logo.

- Try organic food if possible – no harmful insecticides will have been used in its production so your food will not have a harmful effect on the ecosystem.

- Ready meals and convenience food have come about to make our lives easier, especially when we are all pressed for time. However, they come with a high cost in terms of both price and their effect on the environment.

- Look at ingredients – many sweet treats include ingredients that cause damage to our planet, such as palm oil. Try to avoid these.

- Keep a reusable shopping bag by your door so you remember to take it with you to carry your goods home.

- Look out for products that avoid excessive packaging – if you want to make a real statement you can take the packaging off foodstuffs and leave it in the store.

- Take refillable containers to shops – many stores are happy to fill bring-your-own containers.

MAKE THE MOST OF LEFTOVERS

Cooked food can't be composted in your home compost unless you have a special wormery-type composter (a tiered container where worms eat through your kitchen waste). If you don't have room for one of these, you should deal with leftovers the old-fashioned way — by eating them!

One of the easiest and most cost-effective things to do with your dinner leftovers is to pack them up and have them the next day for lunch or dinner. If you are eating away from home, wet leftovers can go in bamboo containers or multi-use plastic lunch boxes, while dry leftovers can be wrapped in beeswax wraps or paper bags.

Leftovers can be chilled and then frozen to be eaten as a quick and easy meal in the future. You can freeze more food than you might expect, including meat, fish, eggs, milk, cheese, rice, bread, fruit and vegetables.

If you eat meat, animal bones can be cleaned, roasted and then boiled with water, herbs and vegetables to create a long-lasting broth or stock. Store the stock in the fridge and use it as a base for soups, casseroles, stews and other rich dishes. Vegetarians or vegans can make stock with similar leftover ingredients, minus the meat!

TOP TIPS FOR
REDUCING FOOD WASTE

- Plan your week's food so that you can make the most of leftovers. For instance, if you have a roast on a Sunday, why not prepare a risotto or soup from leftover ingredients on Monday?

- Batch cook dishes when you have time and freeze food for use at a later date – add the date you made it to the container so you can keep track of when you should use it up.

- Avoid wasting bread by freezing individual slices – don't forget to get them out of the freezer in time for your packed lunches!

- Preserve seasonal food as a treat to eat later in the year – for instance jams, compotes, chutneys and pickles are great ways of using up soft fruits.

- Apples and pears wrapped in old newspaper can be stored in a cool place to extend their edible lifespan.

- Keeping root vegetables such as potatoes, squash and parsnips in a cool, darkened place will preserve them.

- Store onions separately in a cool, dark, ventilated place as they release moisture and gases that cause other vegetables to spoil more quickly.

- Take packed lunches to avoid wasting leftovers.

- Why not give gardening a go? Window ledges are a great place to start growing herb and salad leaf pots, or sprout seeds such as alfalfa for a nutritious addition to a meal.

- Share food with friends, neighbours and colleagues – you could even work out a rota for sharing the week's cooking.

WHAT CAN WE DO ABOUT THE WASTE WE'RE PRODUCING?

A NATION THAT DESTROYS ITS SOILS DESTROYS ITSELF.

FRANKLIN D. ROOSEVELT

Change is coming whether you like it or not.

GRETA THUNBERG

Our earth is bursting at the seams with waste! Our landfills are full and swathes of beautiful earth and ocean are heaped with stinking garbage. The good news is that there is something that everyone can do about it. Tackling the waste issue isn't about cutting it all out — it's much easier than that. The three main ways we can lessen waste are by reducing, reusing and recycling what we have.

You don't have to give up everything you own! Instead, focus on ensuring the products you buy have a small waste impact to start with and then last a long time, being repaired and repurposed when they start to wear out. Find innovative ways of reusing refuse instead of buying from new, and above all recycle efficiently — sometimes a little more time is required to do this effectively.

TOP TIPS
FOR RECYCLING

- Be sure to check for specific instructions on the packaging and only recycle what is recyclable.

- If your locality doesn't recycle a particular material, search online to find out where these items can be taken. This may be a frustrating process but it will be worth it to improve your recycling capability.

- Rinse items before you put them in the recycling: food sitting in bins can render a batch of otherwise good recycling unusable. But don't waste water on washing them until they sparkle: most recycling depots will carry out their own cleaning processes. Ensure your recycling is dry — wet paper and cardboard clogs up the sorting machines.

- Electrical appliances such as toasters, micro-waves, televisions, DVDs, electric toothbrushes, hairdryers, fridges and power tools can be recycled if they are taken to a designated recycling place.

- Hazardous materials such as antifreeze or acid can also be appropriately handled at a recycling depot. Never pour unused chemicals down the drain!

- Finally, make it easy on yourself! Have a small, neat bin or set of bins to store your waste and recyclables: smaller bins make it easier to keep track of the amount of waste you're creating weekly and will help you be aware of what's being recycled and what's going into landfill.

RECYCLE YOUR PLASTIC

Here is a quick guide to the common types of plastic:

- PET or PETE (Polyethylene terephthalate) — mainly clear drinks bottles and some food packaging. Recyclable but not reusable.

- HDPE (High-density polyethylene) — bottles used for things like milk, washing-up liquid and cosmetics. Recyclable and reusable.

- PVC (Polyvinyl chloride) — clear food wrapping, shower curtains and toys. Difficult to recycle.

- LDPE (Low-density polyethylene) — carrier bags, squeezable bottles and four-/six-pack can holders. Currently difficult to recycle, although plans are in place to try to change this. A number of supermarkets take carrier bags for recycling.

- PP (Polypropylene) — cereal bags, bottle tops, margarine tubs, snack bags (for things like potato chips) and straws. Reusable and occasionally recyclable.

- PS (Polystyrene) — packaging for fragile objects and takeout cups. Not reusable and currently difficult to recycle, although plans are in place to try to change this.

- Other — plastics such as acrylic glass, nylon, polycarbonate and items made of a mixture of plastics. Not reusable and difficult to recycle.

AVOID PLASTIC

An important way to cut down on waste is to aim to buy fewer products that include plastic. Did you know that of the 8.3 billion metric tons of plastic has been produced since plastic production started, 6.3 billion metric tons has become plastic waste? Unfortunately, only 9 per cent of that 6.3 billion tons of plastic waste has been recycled. Worse still, around 8 million metric tons of plastic ends up in the ocean every year. The result is that over 100 million marine mammals, and 1 million seabirds die every year due to ocean debris.

Luckily, producers are starting to cut down on the use of plastics in packaging and there are more and more products readily available that reduce its use. You can make your own efforts by seeking products packaged in cardboard or paper, buying loose fruit and vegetables and buying refill products. Remember to always take your own water bottle or flask when you are out and about to avoid buying another plastic bottle.

TOP TIPS
FOR REDUCING WASTE

- Reuse plastic food containers for your own home-made food rather than buying more single-use plastic storage.

- Give plastic bags another use. If they're of the stronger type, put them in your car or bike basket ready for shopping trips. If not, use them for bin liners or take them to a specialist recycling point.

- Use holed or torn plastic bags for crafting – there are plenty of ideas online, from weaving them into baskets to making them into jewellery, bird feeders, art pieces or even rugs.

- If you have unwanted clothes in good condition, give them to friends or donate them to charity to avoid them ending up in landfill.

- Clean tins or cans to use as planters for growing your window-ledge herbs, as a desk tidy to hold pens or you can puncture them with holes and add a tea light to make a lantern.

- Switch to rechargeable batteries – these can be recharged between 500 and 1,000 times and will last for two to three years.

- Use wax cloths instead of single-use plastic film for covering food.

- Reduce the amount of waste coming into your home by cancelling unnecessary mail subscriptions and deregistering from marketing lists – opt for electronic bank statements and circulars instead.

WHAT CAN WE DO AT HOME TO REDUCE OUR IMPACT ON THE ENVIRONMENT?

I WANT YOU TO
ACT AS IF THE
HOUSE IS ON FIRE,
BECAUSE IT IS.

GRETA THUNBERG

What's the use of a fine
house if you haven't got a
tolerable planet to put it on?

HENRY DAVID THOREAU

Once she became aware of the climate crisis, Greta Thunberg urged her family to make small changes in their home to lower their carbon footprint and to make more eco-friendly lifestyle choices. Considering how you use energy and resources in your home is a great way to tackle the question of what you can do to be greener.

Most of us will have to reframe our thinking and some of the new choices we'll make might take a little getting used to. For instance, think of a time when there may have been a problem with the heating in your house, or the water had to be cut off for a short while. It probably seemed like

a real inconvenience at the time, and that's just it — we are used to convenience and sometimes that can make us unaware of how fortunate we already are. Most of us have clean drinking water and warm water to wash dishes and bathe in. We should be grateful for these things, cherish and try not to waste them.

There are many small actions we can take to make a difference within our homes and if everyone commits to making just one small change towards being more eco-friendly, imagine the impact all of those people would have together.

TOP TIPS FOR SAVING ENERGY AROUND YOUR HOME

- Monitor your energy use with phone apps or smart meters – it will help you to see when you are using excessive energy.

- Turn off electrical implements – start with lights. It's all too easy to forget to turn off lights when they are not needed.

- Use eco-friendly light bulbs.

- Unplug and turn switches off at the socket when not in use – you could make monetary savings as well as reducing your energy use.

- Turn the thermostat down – many of us are guilty of overheating our homes.

- Don't rush to put the heating on when it gets colder, start by putting on warm layers and invest in some cosy throws to keep the chill off.

- Make draught excluders to keep your home toasty – an old pair of tights stuffed with newspaper is a simple and effective option.

- Keep the cold out by drawing the curtains.

- Consider getting cavity wall insulation in your home. In the UK, this is offered for free as part of the government's energy saving initiatives.

- Put lids on pans when you are cooking to reduce the time it takes to heat up food.

- Only boil what you need in the kettle – fill a mug and pour this into the kettle to ensure you're not boiling unnecessarily.

- Do your laundry on a cool wash and dry it on a clothes line rather than in a tumble drier.

TOP TIPS TO CONSERVE WATER

There are two types of water usage: direct and indirect. Indirect water usage might include things like using mass-produced materials such as paper and steel. Direct water usage means the water we drink and the water we use to wash our clothes and bodies. Luckily, direct water usage is very easy to manage and reduce.

Here's a list of ideas you can try to cut down your water footprint:

- Use a water-saving device in the toilet cistern.

- Do not flush the toilet every time – "if it's yellow, let it mellow".

- Ensure taps aren't left running unnecessarily – for instance, while brushing your teeth or washing your hands and face.

- Take a shower rather than a bath and take fewer showers.

- Wash your clothes less — another habit we've got into is washing clothes more regularly than necessary.

- If you have to run the tap for any reason, place a bowl underneath it and use the collected water for houseplants or your garden.

- Don't throw away cooking water — some recipes call for a fresh pan of water, but in many cases you could easily reuse it.

- Invest in a water filter to store tap water in the fridge — it'll taste better and will stop you having to run the tap to get cold drinking water.

PAPER'S BETTER THAN PLASTIC, SURELY?

Paper might seem as though it's a fairly eco-friendly product — it's made from trees, right? Yes, and that's just the start of the issue! Some pulp and paper mills use renewable energy and are now fully embracing recycling, using much better practices than in years gone by. However, it's still an incredibly water-intensive industry; in fact, it takes between 5–10 litres of water to produce one sheet of A4 paper. The paper and pulp industry is also energy-intensive, being the fifth-largest consumer of energy in the world. Paper production accounts for four per cent of global energy use.

Deforestation is still an issue for any paper production that isn't sustainable and, even when it is, plantation forests can have their own negative effects on the environment: the effect of such large areas of single crops — creating monocultures — can be devastating to native species.

Paper mills also generate a huge amount of water pollution, use chemicals in their manufacturing process and produce greenhouse gases (though these amounts are far smaller than other major industries). So what can we do?

TOP TIPS FOR CUTTING DOWN ON PAPER CONSUMPTION

- Switch to digital versions of magazines and newspapers.

- Unsubscribe from companies who send you catalogues or junk mail.

- Switch to paperless banking, where you can view all your bank statements and details online.

- Switch to e-books, borrow books from libraries or friends, buy second-hand and pass on your books (including this one!) when you've finished reading them.

- Embrace e-tickets for flights or events and set up your smartphone so you are able to store and view documents online.

- Where possible, ask for digital versions – work documents, receipts, spreadsheets and other paperwork (even contracts and legal documents) can nearly all be viewed just as well on screen rather than as a printed-out version and can be stored forever!

- Avoid printing anything unless you absolutely need to.

- Return junk mail to the sender, letting them know that their unsolicited mail is unwelcome.

- If you must use paper, opt for recycled paper products or buying paper that is regulated and certified by an approved sustainable forest management and legal logging authority, such as the FSC (the Forest Stewardship Council) or PEFC (the Programme for the Endorsement of Forest Certification).

WHY IS WATER CONSERVATION SO IMPORTANT?

Water is a limited resource and its conservation has become a major environmental concern. The effects of global warming loom large when we see reservoirs running dry, hosepipe bans and even limitations placed on domestic water usage in periods of drought. But why has this become such an issue?

Only three per cent of the world's water is drinkable, with the majority of this currently stored inaccessibly within the polar ice caps. And while the amount of fresh water on earth has remained roughly the same through the centuries (thanks to the water cycle's constant recycling), our population is now dramatically bigger than it was even a hundred years ago, meaning resources are under more strain than they have ever been before.

We are also using far more water nowadays for agriculture and industry, putting even more pressure on this precious resource. If we are to avoid a global crisis and save the planet, we need to find ways to effectively manage and conserve our water supplies, and to reduce unnecessary water consumption.

WHAT CAN WE DO IN OUR GARDENS TO HELP THE ENVIRONMENT?

WE HAVE FORGOTTEN
HOW TO BE GOOD
GUESTS, HOW TO
WALK LIGHTLY ON THE
EARTH AS ITS OTHER
CREATURES DO.

BARBARA WARD

Since our leaders are
behaving like children,
we will have to take the
responsibility they should
have taken long ago.

GRETA THUNBERG

Gardens are a great place to retreat for rest and relaxation, but there's so much more they can bring. Not only do the plants they contain do a great job of absorbing harmful carbon dioxide emissions while giving out oxygen in return, but with a bit of a helping hand they can become natural habitats for a raft of environmentally helpful insects. Your garden can play an important role in encouraging biodiversity by creating room for a wide variety of life. Beyond that, it can become a source of food.

If you are lucky enough to have an outdoor area, consider how to use that space and be sure to make the most of it. Those who don't have access to their own garden can look to use community gardens and allotments. There is plenty of information available to help you create an eco-friendly space, from letting your lawn grow wild for a less cultivated insect-friendly area to creating a veg patch.

GROW YOUR OWN

Growing your own food is the best way of eliminating food-based packaging waste and will ensure no harmful chemicals from pesticides are used. If you have a garden you can convert a sunny corner into a veg patch, or use containers and grow vertically in tight spots. Easy wins are crops like tomatoes that are happy to be grown in containers, or why not plant potatoes in disused car tyres stacked on top of each other? Salad leaves are great plants for cropping and regrowing — the vegetable gift that keeps giving.

Home-grown fruit and veg might not be able to completely replace the produce you buy from supermarkets but you should be able to replace a portion of your weekly shop with home-grown ingredients.

Additionally, by growing your own fruit, vegetables and herbs you can guarantee that they are organic and come without the financial and environmental costs of transportation: what you produce can go straight from patch to plate. Replacing just 20 per cent of the food you eat with produce from a home-grown source could reduce your carbon footprint by nearly 32 kilograms (70 lb) of CO_2 per year on average.

TOP TIPS FOR GROWING YOUR OWN

If you are able to plant in your garden, here are a few tips to help you keep things "green" and maximize the eco-benefit of what you grow:

- Select plants that are native. Non-native plants may wipe out native species, potentially unsettling the ecology of your garden and even the local area.

- Choose trees with large leaves and broad crowns, which are the most efficient at absorbing carbon and enabling photosynthesis.

- Grow succulents or alpines. They require significantly less fertilizer and, generally, less water than other kinds of plant.

- Avoid pesticides and opt instead for natural alternatives such as a mix of bicarbonate of soda and water to spray on fungal growth.

- Use recycled materials to grow and care for plants – from planting seeds in cardboard toilet rolls to covering a dormant veg patch with old carpet to prevent weed growth.

- Irrigate with grey water: reuse your kitchen, shower and bathwater for the garden. Do so with care as some detergents can be harmful to your garden.

- Never use peat-based compost.

GET INTO COMPOSTING

Many brands of compost available to buy contain peat, a naturally forming substance found in wetlands like bogs. Unfortunately, the demand for peat-based compost is destroying natural bogs, endangering the habitats and ecosystems that thrive around them — which are critical to biodiversity. Drained bogs also emit greenhouse gases, and every year 630,000 tons of carbon emissions are released due to peat-sourcing.

Half of what the average household sends to landfill is compostable material, mainly from the kitchen. In landfill, food scraps do not compost down as this process requires air. Instead, they rot anaerobically giving off methane gas. This gas helps to trap heat in the atmosphere, leading to global warming and associated climate change. Why not use your waste to make your own compost instead?

If you have a garden, put your food and garden waste in a compost bin or make your own composter.

If you don't have a garden, find or start a "compost collective", whereby multi-dwelling buildings share composting activity. There are also organizations which accept donated compostable waste and will do the job for you.

Aerate your compost once a week by turning the contents over with a garden fork. Worms can be bought or otherwise encouraged into your compost heap to help speed up the process, or you could invest in a wormery.

TOP TIPS
FOR COMPOSTING

Whatever the style of composter you choose, there are techniques that will help you get the best out of your waste. Here are some helpful tips:

- Build your compost pile up from bare earth beginning with a layer of twigs or straw a few inches deep.

- For kitchen waste, composting needn't be a complex process. Take food scraps, peel, leftovers, teabags, coffee grounds and put them aside in a receptacle.

- If the aroma of leftover food is troublesome, keep food scraps in the freezer and empty out once a week for composting.

- Never put any meat, dairy or excrement in your compost heap, as these will lead to unwanted pests and smells.

- Put in fallen leaves, plant and grass cuttings (as long as they don't have diseases), but avoid adding weeds.

- Include black and white newspaper or printer paper. Coloured newspaper and magazines can also be composted so long as they're not covered in wax. Shred your paper before composting to speed up the process.

- Hair (yours or your pet's) is a great source of nitrogen for your compost!

- Fabric that is 100 per cent cotton can be compostable – just remove all adornments and cut into strips. Synthetic fibres do not compost, but cotton rags will decompose in less than six months.

TOP TIPS FOR BRINGING THE WILD INTO YOUR GARDEN

By encouraging wildlife into the garden, you help to achieve a natural balance. Beneficial insects keep pests under control. Birds, amphibians and hedgehogs eat slugs and snails. This does away with the need for chemicals and is better for our health and the environment.

Here are some tips to make your garden a welcome haven for wildlife:

- Hang a bird feeder and leave seeds all year round. This helps those avian species which need support, but also brings biodiversity to your garden. Eco bird feeders are specially designed to utilize materials which are environmentally sound.

- Make the garden hedgehog-friendly. Ensure the perimeter of your garden fencing has holes through which hedgehogs can roam.

- Keep a log pile in a shady corner of your garden — this provides a great habitat for small mammals, amphibians and insects.

- Create your own garden insectarium by growing flowering plants designed to attract and harbour beneficial insects like butterflies.

- Make or buy a bee hotel to encourage these most useful of insects into the garden. You could even consider situating a hive in your green space.

- Do you have room for a pond? If not, consider a birdbath — mammals and birds will find this a useful drinking source, and it will be home to slug-eating amphibians.

TOP TIPS
FOR A GREENER GARDEN

- Apply the same principles to your garden as you would to your household: avoid plastics, select plants and tools with quality and not quantity in mind, reduce waste and try to avoid harmful chemicals.

- Try to choose eco materials in your garden (sourced locally to reduce the carbon footprint of transportation).

- Eliminate chemicals and pesticides which affect the soil composition and enter the water system.

- Employ traditional, natural methods to deal with garden pests, such as eggshells to deter slugs. Peppermint, clove and rosemary essential oils are unpalatable to garden pests.

- Choose permeable materials in your garden, especially in areas of paving and patio. This lessens water run-off and instead allows water to soak naturally into the earth.

- Install a rainwater storage system in your garden – a large container, barrel or water butt that collects rainwater for watering your plants – and avoid using hosepipes and sprinklers.

- Water plants in the early morning or evening to prevent the water evaporating in the heat of the day.

HOW CAN WE REDUCE THE ENVIRONMENTAL IMPACT OF OUR CLOTHING?

AS CONSUMERS WE
HAVE SO MUCH POWER
TO CHANGE THE WORLD
BY JUST BEING CAREFUL
IN WHAT WE BUY.

EMMA WATSON

You must unite behind
the science. You must
take action. You must do
the impossible. Because
giving up can never
ever be an option.

GRETA THUNBERG

The fashion industry does a fantastic job of making us feel the need to buy new items with every changing season and, by producing garments at a price which meets most people's budgets, they make it very easy to do so.

Whether we're buying a new outfit as a treat, for a special occasion or to boost our self-confidence, our seemingly insatiable appetite to constantly refresh our wardrobes comes at more than a monetary cost. What has become labelled as "fast fashion" takes a toll on the environment. Thanks to the multiple stages of manufacturing and transportation for just one garment, the carbon footprint of textile and clothing production is enormous. Even natural fabrics can be problematic.

As with any material possession, the key with clothes is to think about your needs over your desires. With the knowledge that each piece of clothing produced has harmful effects to the planet, stop and ask yourself why you are considering making a purchase — is it a "nice to have" or a "need to have" item? If it's a "nice to have" — for example, something you already own but in a different colour — perhaps consider whether the impact on the planet is worth it. If it's a "need to have" — for example, something to keep you warm and dry — try to make informed choices about your purchases when you shop.

THINK ABOUT THE FABRICS YOU WEAR

Synthetics materials like polyesters are made from petrochemicals, so they are inherently unsustainable; plastic recycled to make clothes might seem like a positive step but microplastics will wash out of them straight back into the ocean. If you can, try to avoid synthetics full stop (rayon, acrylic and spandex are a few more examples).

So, is cotton fabric better? It's a natural plant-based material after all, isn't it? Well yes, but the production of cotton uses vast amounts of water — it takes over 22,730 litres (5,000 gallons) of water to produce enough cotton to create a T-shirt and a pair of jeans.

It is also the most pesticide-intensive crop in the world. Cotton farming takes up a large proportion of agricultural land, much of which is needed by local people to grow their own food.

What about leather? Intensive animal farming plays a role in its production and the tanning and dyeing processes employed to make it wearable are very polluting — not to mention the incredibly inhumane suffering the animals are subject to.

It's a sobering thought to realize the amount of time it takes fabrics to biodegrade once they've been sent to landfill:

Cotton T-shirt — 5 months
Wool socks — 1—5 years
Leather shoes — 25—40 years
Nylon fabric — 30—40 years

ARE THERE ANY ECO-FRIENDLY FABRICS?

Bamboo is often hailed as an eco-fabric. It's a fast-growing grass that, in itself, can be a highly sustainable crop. However, even bamboo is problematic because, like cotton, the most common manufacturing process is highly intensive and involves many harmful chemicals that find their way into the ecosystem.

There's a similar fabric called lyocell that's made from sustainably farmed eucalyptus trees. The same less impactful manufacturing process can be applied to bamboo but it is rare to find this fabric, so there's a way to go before bamboo can truly wear its eco-friendly crown.

Hemp, on the other hand, has good environmental credentials, provided the manufacturing process is sustainable. Made from the stems of flax, jute and stinging nettle plants, this fabric is hard-wearing and sustainable. It requires no pesticides to control and very little water to grow, plus it returns nutrients to the soil.

Whatever fabric you choose, look for organically grown materials as they do not use pesticides and, above all, look for brands that produce sustainable products.

TOP TIPS FOR
DRESSING SUSTAINABLY

- Stop thinking clothes are disposable! Cheap clothes are often far from throwaway as their cost to the earth is immense.

- Stop buying from brands that are careless about the environment. Carry out some online research on the stores you frequently buy from to gain a sense of their ethical approach.

- Try to buy organic fabric and seek out sustainable labels where you'll know the fabric has been produced ethically.

- Purchase pre-loved clothing. Whether you choose to buy second-hand from charity shops or online, there are many bargains to be had, and you'll be giving a clothing item a new lease of life.

- Hand stuff down or give things to charity when you no longer need them rather than simply dumping them.

- Get creative with upcycling — why not turn an old jumper that's lost its shape or has holes in it into a hat, cut up a dress to make a blouse or turn a worn pair of jeans into shorts?

- Extend the wardrobe life of your clothes by repairing items. Learn the art of darning, sew patches, stitch up tears and remove the bobbly bits off jumpers to smarten them up. Local specialists can also help you fix up any worn or damaged clothing.

- Take a leaf out of Greta Thunberg's book and apply the "shop-stop" mentality to your buying habits — don't buy new things unless you absolutely have to and make a point of borrowing from friends or family instead.

WHAT CAN WE DO TO MAKE OUR PERSONAL HYGIENE REGIMES MORE ECO-FRIENDLY?

YOU ARE NEVER
TOO SMALL TO MAKE
A DIFFERENCE.

GRETA THUNBERG

We can't just consume
our way to a more
sustainable world.

JENNIFER NINI

From so-called necessary products like shampoo, deodorant and sunscreen through to cosmetics like face cream and make-up, we get through a massive amount of toiletries. Sadly, most of these everyday products leave a disastrous environmental trail. Not only are dangerous chemicals involved in their production, but the packaging they are presented in is invariably plastic-based and non-biodegradable.

Worse still are hidden dangers. Microplastics are a principal ingredient of many creams and potions that will inevitably make their way from the bottle to the ocean. Microbeads — tiny pieces of plastic added to cosmetic products

such as face wash, toothpaste and abrasive cleaners — were deliberately designed to wash down the drain. The result is that sewerage systems cannot capture them, which means routinely they are flushed through the system into the seas and oceans. Although in some countries bans are in place on the production of microbeads, they can still be found and it's a problem that has already existed for a number of years.

It's time to increase your environmental awareness and make small changes to your personal hygiene regime to avoid the detrimental impact you could be having on the planet.

WHY NOT TRY ECO-FRIENDLY COSMETICS?

Right now, environmentally friendly personal hygiene products tend to be more expensive — as green pressure grows amongst manufacturers, this will hopefully change. However, you need to consider that choosing products made with natural ingredients is generally better for you as well as the environment. Natural products don't include harmful chemicals that can irritate your skin, unlike petroleum-based products — such as lip balm and toothpaste — which use fossil fuels.

If you're just starting out with trialling greener products, take time to carefully read labels to check ingredients and do some research about which brands have products that will suit you and will leave you in safer environmental hands. Sources such as the Ethical Shopping Guide (www.thegoodshoppingguide.com) are an easy way of looking into a company's ethical accreditation.

If you cannot find a natural product to suit your needs or your budget you could try making your own. There are countless reference books and websites that provide information on making your own eco-friendly personal care products.

USE LESS WATER

In the western world we consume an enormous amount of water in our hygiene routine through showering, bathing, and cleaning our clothes. With water being a finite resource, we need to consider ways in which we can reduce our usage. There are some simple ways to do this.

A shower commonly uses between 30 and 80 litres (6.5—17 gallons), while a bath takes up 150 to 200 litres (33—44 gallons). If you only have a bathtub, try a shower attachment or share the bathwater with others. If you have a shower, think about replacing your showerhead.

Quick flow heads and "power showers" pump through water at a faster rate, causing you to use more water over the same shower duration.

Luxurious though it feels to linger beneath the hot water, try timing your shower to reduce the amount of water and energy you use. An eight-minute power shower uses 137 litres (30.13 gallons) of water whereas a five-minute shower using a low-flow showerhead uses only 56 litres (12.31 gallons).

Finally, think twice about whether you actually need a shower — many of us get into habits of showering more regularly than is actually necessary and, unless you do an activity that gets you dirty or sweaty, there's really no need to shower daily.

TOP TIPS FOR GREENER PRODUCTS

- Go completely natural! Why not swap a chemical facial cleanser for coconut oil, petroleum lip salve for soy wax products, or an aluminium-based deodorant for a natural mineral salt version?

- Ditch shower gel in favour of a natural soap and swap liquid for solid shampoo.

- Opt for a natural toothpaste without fluoride – and if you want to avoid plastics or aluminium tubes, toothpaste tablets are easy to buy online and increasingly in stores. Swap your plastic toothbrush for a wooden one with natural bristles.

- Look for ethical and ocean-friendly sunscreen lotions – when swimming in the sea, sunscreen washes off our bodies and enters the water. High amounts of the chemicals from sunscreen have been found on coral reefs: deforming young corals, disrupting their growth and contributing to coral bleaching, which is irreversible.

HOW CAN WE REDUCE OUR CARBON FOOTPRINT WHEN IT COMES TO TRAVELLING?

THE FIRST RULE OF SUSTAINABILITY IS TO ALIGN WITH NATURAL FORCES, OR AT LEAST NOT TRY TO DEFY THEM.

PAUL HAWKEN

The eyes of all future generations are upon you. And if you choose to fail us, I say — we will never forgive you.

GRETA THUNBERG

Transportation generally involves the use of fossil fuels which create carbon dioxide emissions. Staying put and not travelling would be ideal, but that's unrealistic for most of us. The good news is that if we consider how we travel, we can benefit the environment and perhaps save some money too.

The greenest method of transportation depends on how far you have to travel. It's worth researching your carbon footprint compared to the miles you are travelling — there are numerous carbon calculators online to help you do so.

You should always consider the length and necessity of your journey and how quickly you have to be there before you set off. Perhaps there's something that suits your needs closer to home!

MATCHING TRAVEL TO YOUR JOURNEY

SHORT JOURNEYS

Be more mindful about whether or not you need to go somewhere and think about the different options you have. If at all possible, walk where you can. It's all too easy to hop into a car to pick up something you've run out of, but if you start frequently walking for these types of errands you might become better at avoiding unnecessary journeys.

Alternatively, you could try cycling. The bicycle's greenhouse gas emissions are significantly lower than the greenhouse gas emissions created by the average car — even including the emissions created by production and maintenance of each bicycle.

LONGER JOURNEYS

For journeys that are too long to cycle or walk, using buses, trains or trams is your next best bet. These modes of transport are still polluters as typically they use fossil fuels, but mass forms of public transport carry tens or even hundreds of people in a single journey, so they greatly diminish your own personal carbon footprint. Let's face it, the fewer cars on the roads the better — especially those with single occupancy.

If you have to use a car for transport, why not offer others a lift or look into car share schemes? You'll share the emissions with other people, reducing your individual carbon footprints.

TOP TIPS FOR MAKING CAR TRAVEL GREENER

If you do own a car, aim to optimize its performance by the following methods so as to achieve the greatest possible fuel economy:

- Check your car's tyre pressure – underinflated tyres can increase fuel consumption by three per cent.

- Make sure your car gets a regular service – a well-tuned car performs at an optimum level.

- Slow down – observe the national speed limits in place and drive without abrupt stops and starts. Steady, measured driving is more efficient and uses less fuel.

- Don't idle the engine – if you are going to be stopped for longer than ten seconds, turn it off.

- Opening a window for air is marginally better than using air conditioning, but both reduce a car's performance, so reconsider long trips in the heat of the day.

- Travel light – the heavier the load, the more fuel is used. Remove roof racks, as these will cause drag and in turn will consume more fuel.

- When and if you are choosing a new car, consider a hybrid or electric model.

- When washing your car, refrain from using strong chemical cleaners which will wash off into the water system. To conserve water, use a bucket rather than a hose.

TOP TIPS
FOR BIG JOUNREYS

We know that flying isn't great for the environment; aeroplanes burn fossil fuels, emit greenhouse gases and leave vapour trails at high altitude, which all affect our climate. Boat travel can represent a smaller carbon footprint for an individual if loaded to capacity because the fossil fuel cost is shared by a greater number of people, but boats are still polluters.

Here are a few tips to help shape your travel decisions:

- If you are flying, travel direct rather than taking a cheaper but more complicated route — taking off and landing an aeroplane is what uses up the most fuel.

- Consider alternatives – could you reach your destination by train instead and turn it into a railway adventure? Or if it's not a long journey, coaches will be a more energy-efficient choice.

- Unless you're specifically going on a new, efficient and eco-friendly cruise, cruising may have an even worse impact on the environment than other forms of transport. Cruise ships have been criticized for poor waste and water treatment practices which adversely affect the oceans, as well as the damage they can do to the ports where they call, which are often underprepared to receive the large number of day-trippers disembarking from the ships.

Once you've weighed up the travel impact of your trip, you can aim for a more sustainable holiday. There are many beautiful campsites and hotels that are "green", running on renewable energy and waste-free. You can also try eco-tourism, where you spend some time in a stunning location helping locals with green initiatives such as beach cleans or building facilities.

When looking for somewhere to stay, choose places that advocate and employ environmental practices: encouraging recycling, avoiding single-use plastics, following eco-friendly laundry practices, using renewable energy sources, or serving local and seasonal produce in their restaurants. While you're there, don't forget to turn off lights, taps and air-conditioning whenever they're not in use, and try to create as little waste as you can — the locals and the environment will thank you.

Why not go wild? Consider backpacking or walking holidays, staying at local campsites if you want to travel within you own country or region. Or, if you like the idea of a sailing or boating holiday, look for eco-friendly smaller ships with renewable energy sources.

If you are worried about travelling altogether, try a staycation! Research activities that you would not normally do in your local vicinity and have a fun holiday at home.

HOW CAN WE COMBINE GOING GREEN WITH OUR SOCIAL LIVES?

THIS IS NOT A ONE-TIME
THING, THIS IS OUR
ENTIRE FUTURE.

GRETA THUNBERG

The greatest threat to our
planet is the belief that
someone else will save it.

ROBERT SWAN

It's easy to get disheartened and feel as though you'll spend your future missing the things you've cut back on, but that's not the case. You just have to look at life through a different lens and reconsider what really constitutes fun. Good times do not have to revolve around material things, the most treasured memories you can have are from special events or experiences, or when you've simply spent time with loved ones and friends.

Why not consider combining fun with something practical and productive? Spend time with others learning something new — there are so many courses in which you could

get involved on subjects such as ecology, nature, conservation, wilderness safety and survival, animal tracking, organic cooking, wildlife photography and sustainable living.

Give time to charity — the sense of well-being you get from giving is worth it. Get your friends together to volunteer — there are so many events that you can join from litter-picking to beach or river cleaning to tree and hedge planting to volunteering at urban farms. These sorts of activities can seem daunting if you haven't done them before, but you'll soon realize how enjoyable they can be.

GREEN GIFTS

We all love to give gifts, but maybe it's time to rethink the point of doing it. There are countless ideas for experiential gifts on the market, but why not create a home-made voucher, inviting someone to spend time with you?

Alternatively, you could give the gift of giving. There are so many ways you can support charitable causes, from sponsoring a toilet or water treatment facility for a family or community in a developing country, to offering to help set up a school or a community project.

If you prefer to give something physical, buy gifts in charity shops or make your own present. Focus on giving gifts that are edible, reusable or sustainable

TOP TIPS FOR CELEBRATING ECO-STYLE

- Avoid disposable place settings, table decorations, paper plates, cups, placemats and cutlery. Use standard alternatives and just commit to doing a bit more washing-up at the end.

- Use fabric napkins rather than paper ones.

- Ditch items such as balloons, party poppers and glitter sprinkles which all include plastic.

- Do not use Chinese lanterns. They not only pose a fire risk, but the leftover metal parts can also injure wildlife and livestock.

- Decorate your home with items from nature. Paint hens' eggs at Easter. Grow flowers in your garden to cut and display in the summer months. Adorn your home with squashes and pumpkins in autumn. Use eucalyptus, mistletoe, holly and ivy at Christmas. Invest in art made from recycled materials from designers who work with materials discarded by others.

HOW CAN WE MAKE OTHER PEOPLE UNDERSTAND THERE'S A CLIMATE EMERGENCY?

THE FUTURE
WILL BE GREEN,
OR NOT AT ALL.

JONATHON PORRITT

We are striking
because we have done
our homework
and they have not.

GRETA THUNBERG

Becoming an eco-warrior can be hard, especially if you feel as though you are swimming against a tide of negativity. It might seem as though people around you don't care and talking about sustainability can be difficult. However, keep strong as it's very much worth having conversations on the topic, as the more the climate emergency is discussed, the more it becomes part of people's everyday concerns and, with hope, eventually their beliefs will start to change.

Try starting off by talking with friends and family about the efforts you are making in your own life. If you can demonstrate your passion and show them how easy some small changes can be, you could be the inspiration they need to make a positive change.

Be mindful about how you communicate your ideas though — not everyone has the time or ability to be sustainable so never try to force an issue. Instead, lead by example and talk about the positive effects your green actions have on you.

BE AN ACTIVIST

It can make you feel incredibly empowered to have the courage of your convictions. If you want your voice to be heard and you feel it's appropriate for you to get involved in some activism, why not campaign for your beliefs?

After all, school strike days are what 15-year-old Greta Thunberg started. Having spent three weeks striking from school every day by sitting in front of the Swedish Parliament to protest against the lack of action on the climate crisis, she then went on to continue her strike from school every Friday to demand action on climate change. The courage of one schoolgirl was the catalyst for the youth climate movement to evolve. Fridays for Future or Youth Strike for Climate is now a globally known movement with thousands of children striking.

Don't be afraid to stand up for what you believe in, even if some people might make that difficult for you. You might not think that your individual action is important but we cannot assume that others, such as government institutions or corporations, are setting a green agenda, or giving climate change enough priority. Your actions will help others to understand what they can do — be a leader and get others to follow in your footsteps.

TOP TIPS FOR CHALLENGING SCEPTICS

Taking part in activism doesn't necessarily mean tying yourself to a tree or lying in front of a bulldozer! Follow these easy steps to make a small but significant statement about the changes you hope to see:

- Consider which retailers you buy from – align with and buy from those who publish strong sustainability credentials and those who practise what they preach.

- Use and champion companies who agree to accept the return of their own packaging to be reused or request a low- or no-plastic packaging option when you order.

- Ask companies if they routinely have or are able to provide a plastic-free delivery option.

- Question why larger companies insist on sending boxes within boxes. Call out brands and companies who use senseless excess packaging and, if you find excessive packaging is used, flag this up to the retailer or brand, expressing your disappointment. Publicize it.

- Celebrate the good guys by applauding and positively publicizing retailers and brands who manage the packaging problem innovatively, using more sustainable packaging options such as wadding, 100 per cent recycled plastic, 100 per cent recyclable plastic and shredded paper.

- Sign petitions urging policy changes at large companies or in government that will benefit the environment or will put an an end to environmentally harmful practices.

JOIN ENVIRONMENTAL COMMUNITIES

It might sometimes feel like a lonely fight towards climate justice but you needn't feel isolated. There are lots of organizations and charities that are tackling the environmental crisis, and volunteers are always welcome. So why not get involved in activities and join groups? Check online to find out what's happening near you — you'll be amazed at what's on offer: from marine conservation to becoming a tree warden, there's loads to choose from.

If you don't have time to devote to being active within a group you could put your money where your mouth is. If you've been making do with less and have accumulated some savings you could consider donating to charities. There's a wide range to suit many budgets.

Support the green movement with your money by opting to use companies with progressive eco-friendly initiatives and waste-reducing policies in place. You can find lots of information about a company's environmental and ethical standards and policies on their websites.

DON'T LET IT ALL BE DOOM AND GLOOM

Some people don't want to talk about the environment crisis because, let's face it, it's not always a positive point of discussion. Understandably, people might have to confront fear and anxiety and they may not be willing to open up to these emotions. However, it's important to share these feelings and is the first step in making a difference.

You're more likely to engage people in conversations if you can speak about positive action for positive change.

There are a lot of good stories emerging that reflect the invaluable outcome of people's environmental efforts. For example, news about reforestation, or policies being put in place in countries like Canada which aim to protect marine environments by banning oil and gas production. These actions should be celebrated and will encourage the belief that our planet can be saved.

If you come across good environmental news be sure to share it, either in conversation or by spreading the word on social media.

WHAT DO WE SAY
TO THE SCEPTICS?

WHEN HATERS GO
AFTER YOUR LOOKS AND
DIFFERENCES, IT MEANS
THEY HAVE NOWHERE
LEFT TO GO. AND THEN
YOU KNOW YOU'RE
WINNING!

GRETA THUNBERG

I'm often asked whether I believe
in global warming. I now just
reply with the question: "Do you
believe in gravity?"

NEIL deGRASSE TYSON

It's easy to have your head buried in the sand and to overlook the evidence of what's going on in the world. Confronting the truth can be very hard and it's difficult for people to connect with things that they cannot always see on their doorstep. Plus, global, large-scale change that has not yet happened is not easy to get your head around. The problems can seem so large and far away that it would be impossible to change them or unnecessary to care about them with any urgency.

However, there's plenty of evidence available to support what you believe, so make sure you are well informed when you want to prove a point. The best place to start is by sticking to ideas of positive change that you are passionate about — even better to talk about ones that affect you personally and that you are actively involved in being part of. Offer advice that seems attainable and suggest just small changes that your friends and family can start with.

KEEP IT REAL

When you are trying to explain the situation our planet faces, focus on things that people are already experiencing or seeing on the news which they can understand. For instance, extreme weather such as heatwaves, fires, heavy rainfall and hurricanes are becoming more and more common and affect many of us directly. Talking about these events makes it easier for people to connect the tangible effects of climate breakdown to our day-to-day lives.

Talking about likely future events, especially in areas that are currently less affected, brings things to a personal level so that they are easier to understand. For instance, increases in global temperatures of a few degrees won't mean much to the average person but understanding how weather affects them personally might. Focus on the specifics of the area you're in, such as intense rainstorms that cause devastating floods in the UK, increased heatwaves in Europe that have resulted in deaths, or rising sea levels in places like Florida where flooding gets worse year on year.

Start off by asking your friends and family what they know, understand or perceive to be the reality, and how this makes them feel. Try to listen with interest and understanding, and try not to jump in with counterarguments before they've given you their opinion.

Once you understand their perspectives and what information has shaped their understanding you will be better placed to offer a counter-opinion that they might listen to and understand, without simply telling them they are wrong.

Also, if you show that you are compassionate toward someone else's opinions and you're open to having a conversation, you are more likely to find a positive reaction because you are giving that person space to consider their choices.

If you are asked to share your own thoughts and feelings, be honest, but stay calm and be gentle, because the environmental crisis is real, and scary. If you can keep a level head about your opinions you're far less likely to encounter a negative response.

BE READY WITH THE FACTS

Do your research and keep informed so that you can explain to people that scientific evidence is indisputable. There are plenty of websites and blogs that can keep you updated, or you can subscribe to ethical and environmental magazines to keep yourself up to date with the latest information (remember to look out for e-versions of publications).

Above all, keep it personal — discuss what matters to you, as your authentic voice will resonate. When you can understand and articulate your own story, and what personally matters to you, it can help you to find the emotional connection with others and establish common ground. Someone may not be that interested in wildfires on the other side of the world, but they are likely to care about their own homes, families and friends. If you understand yourself and your feelings, you'll find it easier to appeal to this side of people's thinking too.

BEWARE OF ECO-ANXIETY

In all of this you have to be sure to look after yourself physically and mentally. You will no doubt be feeling scared about our climate emergency and you may feel powerless against the enormous task of stopping the problem. Know that you're not alone with these feelings and understand that it's perfectly normal to feel anxious.

If you can try to recognize this fear for what it is, you can share this understanding with others and help them find healthy ways of coping with how they feel and dealing with their mental health.

Working together with others to create a plan of practical things to try, or activities to engage in, will help shift the focus toward doing something positive. Greta Thunberg became apprehensive upon first hearing about climate change — she turned her fear for her future into action, which led her to become the eco-warrior she is today.

Do seek support from friends or family if you are worried that your anxiety levels are affecting your health or from a medical professional if you are seriously concerned about your state of mind.

CONGRATULATE YOURSELF

If you need a pick-me-up, just think you're doing well for even trying. You — just one person — are trying to change the world for the better! Well done!

You are part of a community of like-minded people who are seeking out and embracing ways of living green, discussing positive actions to turn around environments and starting initiatives that are helping thousands of animals and people.

Keep going — it's worth it.

We deserve a safe future. And we demand a safe future. Is that really too much to ask?

GRETA THUNBERG

If you're interested in finding out more about our books, find us on Facebook at Summersdale Publishers and follow us on Twitter at @Summersdale.

Thanks very much for buying this Summersdale book.

www.summersdale.com